D0953755

ONE LARK, ONE HORSE

MICHAEL HOFMANN

FARRAR, STRAUS AND GIROUX

NEW YORK

Farrar, Straus and Giroux
120 Broadway, New York 10271

Title-page illustration courtesy of Barbara Hoffmeister.

Grateful acknowledgment is made to the editors of the following publications,
where some of these poems first appeared: *Australian Book Review*, *La Errante*,
Grand Street, *Granta*, *Heat*, *London Review of Books*, *The Nation*,
The New Yorker, *The New York Review of Books*, *1914: Poetry Remembers*,
The Paris Review, *Ploughshares*, *Plume*, *Poetry*, *The Poetry Review*, *Raritan*,
The Spectator, and *The Times Literary Supplement*.

Library of Congress Cataloging-in-Publication Data
Names: Hofmann, Michael, 1957 August 25– author.
Title: One lark, one horse : poems / Michael Hofmann.
Description: First American edition. | New York : Farrar, Straus and Giroux,
2019.
Identifiers: LCCN 2019000368 | ISBN 9780374226596 (hardcover)
Classification: LCC PR6058.O345 A6 2019 | DDC 821/.914—dc23
LC record available at https://lccn.loc.gov/2019000368

Our books may be purchased in bulk for promotional, educational, or business
use. Please contact your local bookseller or the Macmillan Corporate and
Premium Sales Department at 1-800-221-7945, extension 5442,
or by e-mail at MacmillanSpecialMarkets@macmillan.com.

www.fsgbooks.com
www.twitter.com/fsgbooks • www.facebook.com/fsgbooks

1   3   5   7   9   10   8   6   4   2

Thanks: For a conversation he won't remember, Jeremy Harding. For the kind
use of her name on top of the piece she commissioned, Lindsay Garbutt. For
encouragement, support, curiosity, also forbearance, sometimes over many
years: Barbara Hoffmeister, Jonathan Galassi, Matthew Hollis, Alan Jenkins,
Larry Joseph, Ange Mlinko, André Naffis-Sahely, Robin Robertson, Frederick
Seidel, Don Share, Julian Stannard, George Szirtes, Rosanna Warren.

Of course he was very witty and funny when he was happy, and loved to tell her Jewish jokes and stories; like the one about Goldberg and Cohen, who have delicatessen shops next to each other. Goldberg's shop (he recounted) is always packed, while Cohen's is empty; so finally Cohen asks his friend what on earth he is selling. 'Lark pâté,' Goldberg tells him. 'Lark pâté?' gasps Cohen. 'But how can you afford it?' 'I add a bit of horse,' Goldberg replies. 'How much?' 'One lark, one horse,' says Goldberg.

CAROL ANGIER, *The Double Bond: Primo Levi—A Biography*

The adjective has come back, after its ten years' exile.

GEORGE ORWELL, *"Inside the Whale"*

Stop trying to be a poet. There's no time.

NAGUIB MAHFOUZ

Contents

ONE LARK, ONE HORSE

Lindsay Garbutt

I'm past the age of reading, and well into the age of re-reading. I know, because I hated my father for it when he did it. And I don't re-read either. About eight months ago, I started buying reading glasses. I have three pairs, which I variously use and don't use. I've never had glasses before. I was the boy who saw the buffalo a mile away. A piece I wrote last summer about Brecht was my first with glasses. I avoid putting them on as much as possible, because they make the rest of the room disappear. Now I have another piece about Brecht to write. I'm an inefficient volcano. Half-remembered scraps of things come out of my head. I don't know what book I last read, except for purposes of reviewing or translating. "Do you have that in a large type edition?" Admission: I read Leon Wieseltier's piece in *The New York Times* about our virtualized post-human scientistic predicament. The Internet seems to have killed off pictures, writing, and music at one fell swoop, which isn't bad going for one lousy money-spinning invention. I thought that was probably the best synoptic article I've read for ten years, or whenever *The Guardian* had a piece about a nasty practice called "astroturfing." The world is so full of false accounting and conniving. All vampires and zombies, if you ask me. It gives one conniptions. I put on John Cale's *Paris 1919* this morning, and sat there in floods of tears. That mixture of prettiness and geography and bottleneck guitar does me in. And Lowell George and Ritchie Hayward are dead. Nothing post-human there. And when I last saw John Cale he had pink hair and a goatee. I wonder what he was reading.

The Years

Nothing required an account of me
And still I didn't give one.

I might have been a virtual casualty,
A late victim of the Millennium Bug.

No spontaneity, no insubordination,
Not even any spare capacity.

LV

The luncheon voucher years
(the bus pass and digitized medical record
always in the inside pocket come later,
along with the constant orientation to the nearest hospital).
The years of "sir" (long past "mate," much less "dearie"),
of invisibility, of woozy pacifism,
of the preemptive smile of the hard-of-hearing,

of stiff joints and the small pains
that will do me in. The ninth complement
of fresh—stale—cells, the Late Middle Years
(say, 1400 AD—on the geological calendar),
the years of the incalculable spreading middle,
the years of speculatively counting down
from an unknown terminus,

because the whole long stack—
shale, vertebrae, pancakes, platelets, plates—
won't balance anymore, and doesn't correspond anyway
to the thing behind the eyes that says "I"
and feels uncertain, green and treble
and wants its kilt as it climbs up to the lectern to blush
and read "thou didst not abhor the virgin's womb."

The years of taking the stairs two at a time
(though not on weekends)
a bizarre debt to Dino Buzzati's *Tartar Steppe*,
the years of a deliberate lightness of tread,
perceived as a nod to Franz Josef
thinking with his knees and rubber-tired Viennese *Fiaker*.
The years when the dead are starting to stack up.

[6]

The years of incuriosity and *novarum rerum
incupidissimus*, the years of cheap acquisition
and irresponsible postponement, or cheap
postponement and irresponsible acquisition,
of listlessness, of miniaturism, of irascibility,
of being soft on myself, of being hard on myself,
and neither knowing nor especially caring which.

The years of re-reading (at arm's length).
The fiercely objected-to professional years,
the appalling indulgent years, the years of no challenge
and comfort zone and safely within my borders.
The years of no impressions and little memory.
The years of "I would prefer not"
and "leave me in the cabbage."

The years of standing in elevators
under the elevator lights in the elevator mirror,
feeling and looking like leathered frizz,
an old cheese-topped dish under an infrared hot plate,
before they kindly took out the lights
and took out the mirror, and slipped in screens
for news, weather, and sponsors' handy messages.

The years of one over the thirst
and another one over the hunger, of insomnia
and sleeping in, of creases and pouches and heaviness
and the barber offering to trim my eyebrows.
The years of the unbeautiful corpse in preparation.
The years to choose: *sild*, or *flamber*
. . . ?

Daewoo

Heavy, and now grizzled (*pro tem*) and generally high
  colored.
The voice light, tripping over itself, setting off at an angle
into the thickets of vocabulary. It's gone; let it go.
No one knows I stole (wonder how?) Alan Waugh's
  chewed voice
when I was seventeen. Piling out of the car,
my *Siebensachen* on the tarmac, my rucksack upside
  down,
the small size of bulldog clips everywhere.
Forty years of chaotic exits, and now one more.

Derrick

That rather sprawling
foursquare spelling. Always
in my mind half-
associated with the hirsute
14-year-old I saw
in the newspaper
who sued his local

education authority
to keep his beard,
out of a sort of medical
necessity. My neighbor
took up residence
next to this youth
in my head. Derrick.

Clean-shaven, Welsh,
heavyset, lugubrious,
his steel-gray hair
apparently parted
by a steel comb.
Tracksuit bottoms,
graphite racket, retired

from something or other,
maybe ex-army.
A plangent sonorousness.
If I have it right,
India. A grandfather
in spe, then fact.
He was shy, I was shy.

At the height of things
he fed me clippings
from the *Telegraph*,
and we talked about
militaria (I was translating
Ernst Jünger—
though not in time for him).

Some village-y gene
had given him
the atavistic habit
of standing outside
his front door for hours
arms crossed,
surveying the scene.

Perhaps a swagger stick
to take the parade.
He knew the street
as I didn't know him,
spent years setting plants
and persecuting graffiti
in a tiny doggy flowerbed

under the railway bridge,
played tennis
on the corporation courts,
kept an ear open
for the local scuttlebutt.
Like a hardy perennial
he stood there

under his wife's hollyhocks—
now both under the ground,
massive heart attack (he),
years of chemotherapy
at the Royal Free and Easy (she),
buried from St. Dominic's
down the road,

the orphaned court,
the problematic flowerbed
improbably flowering,
the neighbors shuffling past
the hollyhocks (pink),
more local connections
than I'll ever have.

Smethwick

"What changed? Same maisonette in West London,
the straight shot of Talbot Road, held on to in spite
    of everything—
one's original intended went away, someone else
    eventuated—
riding to work on the Tube like an Edwardian, same
    job, steady Eddie,
not 'a new kind of tobacco at eleven,' and 'my love
returning on the four o'clock bus,' more 'cut out the
    ciggies'
and a new palliness. Hamlet for yonks, kicked upstairs,
Prospero under this bonkers management."

Portrait d'une Femme

The age demanded an image
Of its accelerated grimace
EZRA POUND

You were energized by your epoch.
The difference between a harmless nut—John Doe, Jane
   Doe, plain Jane,
practically any mediocrity—standing on a beach
and the same harmless nut
riding a wave of (now) cultural self-righteousness
about to tube. A tsunami armed with thunderbolts.
Empowered—yea, packing.

You played everything to the sympathetic studio theater
of your hearers, a chorus–cum–sounding board.
They were your doo-wop boys and girls,
your clique and claque and Marshall stack. The church
   hall chairs scraped,
the cheap black crêpe backdrop rustled "cutting edge"
   at you.
You paid attention to how they oohed and aahed for you,
and then pantomime hissed, and balled their fists and
   bayed for blood:

the half-lustful half-men betraying their half-gender
when they weren't speculating what you were like in bed,
the frightened girls who'd never seen anything like you
but thought it might be fun (after Goth) to be a Maenad,
the Pharisaic mothers going home to their chilly fires,
their dim, furtive, put-upon husbands and their neo-feral
   offspring
with a "There but for the grace of God" on their bony lips.

[13]

And it was all you, the decisive impulse, the focus, the
     leadership;
why, there was the beef, right there with its bleeding foot
     in its mouth.
The venomous articulation with its trademark solecisms
(naive to wonder how anyone with a Cambridge degree
     in it
could hurt the language like you).
A sort of chronically overemphatic sub-style of maimed
     English,
a testosterone debris of nursery babble, pop psychology,
     tabloid yelp, and obscenity.

Strangers were helpless in its vortices,
lawyers needless to say loved it—
what they would have given (M'lud) to be able to solicit
     like that.
It was all as humdrum as graffiti, vivid and appalling
and unutterably humdrum, it was Mary Elizabeth
Bott in the William books going
"I'll thcweam and thcweam and *thcweam*."

It's strange, you were ungainly, but you were never
     wrong.
You had the yessers and nodders and eggers-on
to take care of that. Ungainliness in this instance
happened to be the price of rightness.
You espoused ungainliness. Worshipped it.
Ungainliness was the new duty. The new beauty.
Disinhibition ruled. Wa-hey.

And so it somehow had to be. You did it for them.
You erupted out of Englishness and made an exhibition
   of yourself.
(Tiny *terremoto* in Derby that I read about in Mexico,
   2 point something on the Richter scale.)
Once it might have been said where you came from you
   forgot yourself,
but that style of rebuke went out of fashion. Anyway,
   you weren't into
forgetting yourself. You were into remembering yourself.
As you would have said, 24/7.

It would have been good to do smolder like Anna
   Magnani
or have a wronged profile like Dante's, whoever the fuck
   Dante is.
But you couldn't hack that.
So you chucked glasses and went public.
Bridget Jones thuggee. Jordan *tragédienne*.
The English rose goes ape.
Deal or no deal.

You were good value at cocktail parties. For about five
   minutes.
Then you were a bore; and as the good book didn't say,
   the bores are always with us.
You would have loved a column like Margaret Cook.
   (Not a cooking column.)
Your mother was dead, your godmother was dead,
look what happened to them. (They died.)
Perhaps there was something you could do,
and so you stayed alive and humbly served the numpties.

Stag Party, Tallinn, May

"Umlauts and double vowels. The pale stares of Estonians.
Sex workers. I wish they all could be. Marriage industry
   execs,
More like. Baltic brides. Clothes short, scant, tight, and
   bright.
A predilection for things long buried in the ground.

An unusual proliferation of maimings and disfigurements.
Pathos in monumental sculpture. Lilac in the offing.
Polyethnic, also Cyrillic. Old Believers over the water.
British booze cruisers. There's nothing to touch breasts."

Judith Wright Arts Centre

My office! My office at the Judy! The Judy
at the head of Fortitude Valley—Happy Valley!—
the ex-tea and -coffee warehouse, but reformed,
    reformed!
The industrial brick carcass full of arty bees,
sphinx of a building couchant on the crest of the hill,
the infrared elevator mysteriously redolent of cloves,
restaurant smuggled into one corner, cafe in another,
and the whole dipped in chocolate and tile.

The walk along Brunswick Street to my office
up two hills and down two dales—why every town in
    Australia
has to have a street named for Hessian mercenaries
I don't know—past the absurdly good coffee shops
and the absurdly good ice-cream parlors
and the absurdly good banks, the backpacker hostels,
the ethnic restaurants, the skin clinics
and fitness studios and chiropractors and nail bars.

A touch about it of DHSS and Camden Town,
a touch of Prenzlauer Berg, and then always a touch
of paddle steamer, the tropical levity conferred
by the tracery balconies and louvers and pillarets,
the rusting roofs and riotous growth;
taking in the trees as they went red and blue
and the stumps of the succulents spurted buttercream,
and the whiff of mock orange and jasmine and chips.

The bookshop no longer, and the cinema no longer
and the theater a fishbar theatrically named The Codpiece
but still the surprisingly earnest and massive hotels,
intemperance hotels, and one music venue after another,
and all of them *Spelunken* and grotto dark,
and the endearing bars with their windows wound down,
and the customers staring out at the continuous *paseo*
of the young, the buxom, the drapey, the stringy:

the pre-owned and the pre-loved, the much-traveled
and the want-away, the ripped and the buff
and the sweatered and coated, the baby-dolled and the
    muscle-shirted
and the skirts pulled over trousers and leggings,
and the flip-flops and biker boots, and tote bags and
    shoulder bags
strapped across the bosom. (And it was all one style,
and the name of that style was called Alternative, or
    maybe,
Consensual Alternative at the World's End.) The Judy.

The little nest—suite—of three or four subdivided rooms
—that plasterboard and aluminium arrangement
so relatively permanent in its provisionality—
the red daubed walls and purple foam sitcom furniture.
My office—hardly ever used in anger—though I did stuff
a thousand pages of *Alone in Berlin* into a cake box for
    collection once,
and then surfed home down ten blocks of Brunswick
    Street,
out of the green sky of the short northern dusk.

(Brisbane)

Cricket

Another one of those Pyrrhic experiences. Call it
an ex*pyrrh*ience. A day at Lords, mostly rain,
one of those long-drawn-out draws so perplexing to
     Americans.

Nothing riding on the game, two mid-table counties
at the end of a disappointing season, no local rivalry or
     anything like that,
very few people there, the game itself going nowhere
     slowly

on its last morning. The deadest of dead rubbers.
Papa had his beer, but you two must have wondered
     what you'd done wrong.
Did I say it was raining, and the forecast was for more
     rain?

Riveting. A way, at best, for the English
to read their newspapers out of doors, and get vaguely
     shirty
or hot under the collar about something. The paper,
     maybe, or the rain.

Occasionally lifting their eyes to watch the groundsmen
     at their antics—
not just hope over experience but hope over certain
     knowledge.
It was like staying to watch your horse lose.

And yet there was some residual sense of good fortune
    to be there,
perhaps it was the fresh air or being safely out of range
    of conversation
or the infinitesimal prospect of infinitesimal
    entertainment.

One groundsman—the picador—mounted on a tractor,
others on foot, like an army of clowns, with buckets
    and besoms.
The tractor was towing a rope across the outfield
    to dry it—

we saw the water spray up, almost in slow motion—
as from newly cut hair. The old rope was so endearingly
    vieux jeu.
It approached a pile of sawdust—two failing styles
    of drying—

and one of the groundsmen put out his foot to casually
    flick it over,
as sporting a gesture as we expected to see all day
in terms of finesse, economy of movement, timing.

He missed, and instead the rope sliced right through the
    sawdust pile,
and flattened it. A malicious laugh, widely dispersed
    and yet unexpectedly hearty,
went up on all sides of the ground. Soft knocks that
    school a lifetime—no?

Letter from Australia

to Ralph Savarese

The early worm gets the bird—
it's morning in Australia.
It's strange to be so bilious
so far away.

Little to do with Australia,
which so far as I can see
seems mostly delightful:
airy pastel buildings and trees I can't name.

There is some peculation
among the local pols,
mainly relegated to the business section:
a few million hectares rightly or wrongly
    grazed or mined.

The shilly-shallying of Costello (who has a
    book to sell-o),
the ill-mannered couple at the Iguana,
the chair-sniffer unluckily caught in the act,
a victim of his own special brand of gallantry.

Then there was the recent South Sea shindig
all in matching shirts and kilts,
except for poor Fiji, which
was sent to Coventry.

The local parliament yammers all day—
you can get used to the phantom
pinpricks of short "i"s in words
like beach, bush, or bake—

and then the Beeb burbles all night
dreaming to itself in Queen.
And when we wake up,
the world is still spoiled

by the comical malfeasance
of its whilom last best hope,
the familiar American *galère*
fourteen hours abaft of us:

Cheney the sinisterly skewed orangutan,
the worn charmlessness of Bush,
the clumping one-armed snowman McCain,
looking either to club or hug.

And now—the commentariat agog
at the promised mélange of snow sports
    and water sports—
Sarah P., the driller killer,
the uterine shooterine.

The "real" routinely trumping "politics"
—as if politics weren't real.
There are no more anchovies,
but there is still fishing and (apparently)
    Anchorage.

If you can have little Englanders,
can't you have little Americans,
half-awash with Washington's hormones,
half in rebellion against them.

The imprisoned balloons
in the false ceiling of the "Palindome,"
hang above the fat freed faces.
Cyclothymia in the USA.

My friend in the bonsai liberal exclave
in your biodiesel flyover state,
I can still register my first
Zolaesque frisson of horror

at the fried turnip smell of the cars
that ate not Paris, but whatever you called it—
I Oughta Went Around it.
There is no going around it.

Old Mexico

They can't get enough of the indecent
toy skeletons *in copulo* every which way,
the perpetual action heroes, the cast-off clothes
with writing on them, the *mufla*

and *vulcanizadora* shops, the girls in bathtub jeans
from no label they ever heard of,
no film without Schwarzenegger or Willis,
wrought iron and tin mirrors, sad tenor crooners

over brass, *caja de ahorros* (chamber of horrors),
joyerias (brothels), the prettier the place
the uglier the music, the men growing more and more
like themselves, the women more and more like the men,

an orange balancing on an orange
balancing on an orange, no dry stick poking
out of the ground without a flower, and those
flagrant skeletons—like there's no tomorrow.

Recuerdos de Bundaberg

for Chris Wallace-Crabbe

No, I don't remember Guildford
ROBYN HITCHCOCK

Did I fly there? I may have flown there.
Maybe in something with the specifications of a crop
    duster.
The Sugar Coast. Everything comes with a name.
    A name and a nickname.
The Soaked Coast. Bundy. Blue rustle of cane. Home to
    Rum City Wrecking.
[Farewell,] Bundaberg, Home of Bricks. Big Daddy's
    Pies. Hair Force One.

And the nature. Grass trees, wedding bushes, acid frogs,
    termite nests.
Beaded or bearded dragons. Together or separately,
    I don't remember.
I saw one, though, it was huge, in some undergrowth.
Harmless, probably, but ferociously ugly.

I left the workshop in the Rotary Club. I took the Bra
    Challenge,
or did not take the Bra Challenge. I headed down
    Bourbong Street.
Toward the Bennett or the Burnett (the sources are
    unclear).
One of those short catastrophic Australian rivers.
    The old bones of sugar refineries.
The pocked mud glistening with thousands of alert little
    mud crabs.

The farmers came in to buy dry goods and do their
    banking and get soaked.
The mercantile brick paving, awnings, shade, and
    a gentle breeze.
Horace would have appreciated it. *Amoenus*, I can hear
    him saying.
The twentieth century, the Wild East.

I occupied an array of public benches. Hours went by.
Chinese tourists mooched disconsolately down the
    pavements. *Sol* or *sombra*, to taste.
The Mediterranean social life of lorikeets. The inverted
    magpies.
The Golden Basket, the Golden Casket, the Golden
    Gasket.
Three for the price of four.

Bundaberg. Somewhere I'd no reason to be.
Anywheresville, as in miles from.
No dot on a marconigraph, semicolon, on no radar
    a single ping.
Or if there was, then just a ping singing to itself.

see something say something

Imaginary man, go.
DAN PAGIS

every transparent man his own bar-
code his own passwords account
activity iris scan fingerprints
tribal/maiden name payment
history gold/silver/platinum/
lead cards ID (non-drivers incl.)
mobile number(s) email
addresses medical records
organ donor card insurance
allergies next of kin pets
police record age next birth-
day employer's letter tax
number implants joint re-
placements cranial plate
pacemaker social network
aliases chat rooms mother's
birthday and middle initial

welcome on board unusual
activity prior religious affili-
ation GSOH soul patch smell

Before she met me

after Ovid

There was the narcoleptic giant,
the absentee clotheshorse,
the petrified virgin, and the flaky sadist.
Then she met me.

Cavafy: *Subrosa*

Both of us disposable/so disposed/at each other's
    disposal,
so put me away, have me ejaculate against your hip
as part of some exhaustive totalizing method,
        leave the children with someone
        ("make the necessary arrangements"),
park around the corner at some ungodly hour twenty
    years ago,
give the barest touch on the doorbell, hush, and tiptoe
    down
to the blue daybed with your hair electric from the cold.

Hudson Ride

ich weiss nicht, was soll es bedeuten
HEINRICH HEINE

Red and yellow bittersweet; Poughkeepsie;
the ice jags are silver, rush spikes gold
in the blue December. A big old eagle,

white head, white feet, perches on a tree
like a postage stamp or a glorified house cat.
Socks *in excelsis*. —God, what is it with separation?

A soft freeze. The woods are rusty stone, henna fuzz
    ravines,
snow slicks. Ice blinds and dries. Dazzles and steams.
Swans outside Croton. I sit in the train,

at the very back of the last car,
ruing every mile. Some sort of folly and exhilaration.
A caffeinated feeling of being all heart.

"Shouldn't I ask to hold to you forever." I rather think I
    did ask.
They thought it was the New Rhine, here, or wanted to.
Rhinebeck. Germantown. Dutchess County.

My girl, someone's girl, her own girl. Perhaps
the only other time in my life I've opposed the machinery
and scale of the world. My personal insurrection.

Auflehnung. A leaning up against—say, and by preference,
you in your kitchenette and sweater among the hi-hats
and bolt cutters and beheaded pin sculptures.

Now here come the hard options: the cracked old
    Nabisco plant,
West Point, Indian Point, Ossining, Rockland Psych.,
Drachenfels. Bacharach. Loreley. Loreley. Loreley.

Baselitz & His Generation

for Hai-Dang Phan

I have no doubt where they will go. They walk
the one life offered from the many chosen.
ROBERT LOWELL

They are all also, it should be remembered, West German artists,
with the partial exception of Penck, and are all male.
JOHN-PAUL STONARD

He was born in the countryside/the provinces/the
  blameless sticks
            in (*false*) Waltersdorf (*recte*) Dresden
            in what is now Czechoslovakia/the Czech
               Republic (*laughs*)/Czechia,
                              if it ever catches on
            what's it to you.

Stripped of his East German citizenship, he fled
            on foot with a handful of pop music cassettes
            in a pantechnicon *mit Kind und Kegel*
            in pandemonium
            nach vorne
            cool as you like, in an S-Bahn from the
               Russian Sector, in the clothes he stood up in.

Germany (thus Goethe's friend Mme de Staël) is the
   land of poets and thinkers
            der Dichter und Denker
            or of judges and executioners
            der Richter und Henker
            or of Richter and Penck.

[32]

He drew innocent geometrical shapes
       boxed shirts/boxer shorts/boxy suits
       men without women
       hairy heroes of the Thirty Years' War/
          lansquenets/strangely fibrous figures a bit
          like those *New Yorker* caveman cartoons
       empty Renaissance helmets/mostly U.S.
          fighter jets
       the suicides of Stammheim.

He took the name of an American boxing promoter
       a German Ice Age geologist
       the village of his birth
       the one he was given.

His first work to really catch on/be banned/get him in
   trouble/cause widespread revulsion was *Onkel Rudi*
       Die grosse Nacht im Eimer
       Höhere Wesen befahlen: rechte obere Ecke
          schwarz malen!/oyez, oyez,
              oyez, Politburo decree: upper right
                hand corner in ebony!
       ohne Titel
       a mural in the cafeteria of the Hygiene
          Museum, since painted over.

He wound up in Düsseldorf
       Berlin, *doh!*
       la bella Italia
       tax-exempt Ireland of Böll- and Beuys-full
          memory, where the earth-apples bloom.

His paintings were fuzzy geometry
        like the country, ripped across the middle
        upside down (especially effective: the trees)
        shoveled out of the window
        later withdrawn.

His favored technique involved stick figures
        Polke-dots
        out-of-focus *grisaille* photographs
        scribbling on his pictures
        woodcuts à la Dürer.

The numerals on his graphics represent a recent
  shopping bill
        an attempt to disconcert the onlooker/
          Ostranenie
        amortization
        bar code
        some other code
        Durchnummerierung.

He studied with Joseph Beuys
        the least doctrinaire painter he could find
        for the best part of ten years, in East and
          West, so that everything canceled itself out
        what's it to you
        he didn't.

Fontane

for Jan Wagner

Acacias. Acacias and rain make May here, the way
lindens and rain make July. Layers of complication and
    sorrow,
which precipitate as opinion. Brusque. Off-kilter.
    Uncalled-for.
A long and hopelessly trammeled backstory. Midnight.
The biggest brick church in the whole of Brandenburg.
Two burly men head off into the park with their
    impossibly tiny dog.

Sankt Georg

Sankt Georg, what was it, questionable, doubtful,
    shady, twilit,
a something area, something Jan said, and he was born
    in Hamburg,
and went to school here, so he would know.

A little isthmus between the Alster with its freshwater
    sailors
and the railway station, always a reliable drag on things
    anywhere in Europe
(the transients, the drugs, the pre-set collisions between
    the foolish young

and the unscrupulous old), though this one piped
    classical music—not anymore—
to the forecourt, where taxi drivers got out
and walked their Mercs around in neutral

because they were hours without a fare and were saving
    diesel
(which was all very well in summer),
and the immediate, somehow always slightly grubby or
    compromised view

of three theaters, two museums, and le Carré's bunker
    hotel,
but, hey, it was classy while it lasted,
and you could get to Milan or Moscow if you had to.

Then the *Polizeibezirk* of underage *Puppenstrich* about
    the time
B. came here from the country,
still often the only girl not on the game, among whores

and winos and people "with an immigration background"
looking grim and wearing sub fusc and doing the
    messages, as we once said. Then gays—
is there a pink euro, like a pink pound, and the Pink
    Pistols and Grey Wolves?—

intrepid advance guard of gentrification.
So up the rents, send in the heavies, firebomb the
    buildings, locals out,
make improvements, and up the rents again, same
    everywhere.

A natty pellucid pissoir in the Hanser Platz that it
    would take Paris to pull off,
drunks round the monument ("reel around the
    fountain"), hardy trees and hardier women,
little roosters, little rosters in the apartment block for
    cleaning the common parts,

little brass squares set in the ground for individual
    fascist outrages,
with the victims' names, the massy church at the end
    of the street—
St. George's, the AIDS church, the rainbow flag,

the fire-breathing community paper called the *Dragon*.
Sudden sad flurries of flowers, the curt pairs of dates,
a grown-out bleached person with one leg.

The main drag changed utterly,
meaning as usual stylistic diktat from elsewhere
and the birth of an interchangeably frippish
    hideousness. Three hat shops,

an empty tea bar (tax write-off? money laundry?)
    boasting sixteen varieties of macaroons,
endless places to stop (if you even wanted to stop)
    on the narrow pavement
between the heedless cars and the nosy passersby,

expensive ready-cooked food shops with names like
    Mom's, gone
the hardware store that stocked everything and was
    staffed by people
who advised you where to find it for even less, out of
    business,

or moved away to less promising parts.
The photo shops, the record store, bookshop. All gone.
And behind that, the Steindamm, our belly and balls,

twinned with Kabul, or Mombasa, or Abuja.
Telephone shops if you wanted to call anywhere with
    a red, green, and black flag
(launchpad of Ali Ağca and his crew of martyrs),
    casinos,

thorny or hairy vegetables, fetish stores, Alphonso
    mangoes from Pakistan,
video brothels, limitless mint and parsley and cilantro,
    hourly hotels,
cracked olives and fresh cheese, old girls with three
    words of German, newly baked flatbread.

The birds strike up between three and four (it's the
   northern light),
while at lit intersections they never stop.
Twilit, doubtful, shady, questionable. Something.

Night

It's all right
Unless you're either lonely or under attack.
That strange effortful
Repositioning of yourself. Laundry, shopping,
Hours, the telephone—unless misinformed—
Only ever ringing for you, if it ever does.
The night—yours to decide,
Among drink, or books, or lying there
On your back, or curled up.

An embarrassment of poverty.

F.S.

In bed
with Fred;
hugger-mugger
with *Ooga-Booga*.

Broken Nights

for Bill and Mary Gass

Then morning comes,
Saying, "This was a night."
ROBERT LOWELL

Broken knights.
—No, not like that.
Well, no matter.
Something agreeably
Tennysonian (is there
Any other kind?)
About "broken knights."
Sir Bors and Sir Bedivere.
In my one-piece pajamas—
My it-doesn't-matter suit,
With necessarily nonmatching
—Matchless, makeless, *makeles*—
Added top, I pad
Downstairs to look
At the green time
On the digital microwave.
My watch, you must know,
Died on my watch
All at the top, at midnight,
After a few
Anguished weeks of macro-
biotic Stakhanovite
5-second ticks,
And I haven't had
Time, it seems,
To get it repaired.
Further (weewee hours),

To patronize
My #2 bathroom *en bas*
(Though N.B.
Only for a pee).
Groping for a piss,
As the poet saith.
Wondering how soon
It might be safe
To turn on the wireless,
Without it being either
New Age
Help you through the night
Seducer mellotrons
(What's a tron, mellow I can do?)
Or merely
Dependency inducing
And *wehrzersetzend*,
Deleterious for morale of the troops.
I eat to the beat,
Then snooze to the news.
Drift off to *Morning Edition*.
Arise/ Decline, Sir
Baa Bedwards.

For Adam

In that aftertime
I wasn't writing. I never wrote,
I didn't know what the aftertime was for.
I felt little, collected nothing.

I talked to myself, but it was boring.

Warszawa

Chipping at frozen puddles.
Magpies and varieties of crow.
The halt and the blind.

All day in the bakery.
The rise of the muffin.
Res sacra miser.

The sacred business of pity.
Ministries. Hotspots.
The Chinese Embassy.

Raw sienna and burnt umber.
Brick and stucco.
Strawberry and vanilla.

Lean and fat, roof and wall.
Statues with swords.
Statues with lances and canes.

Profligates, ascetics, martyrs.
Stomatologia to *apteka* and back.
Lourdes next 7 exits.

Dead Thing

A dead thing floated downriver in Tartu.
At first I thought it was wood,
A rotting bole, some vestigial sharpness and strength.
An upside-down coffee table, with claws,

Imperturbable. Inflated, like a flotation device.
A head end and a tail end, but a
Certain amount of discretion, like a tortoise.
But dead. Under the willows a carcass.
Purposefully downstream, like a blond in the twenties.
    Mahogany dead.
    Laced football dead.
    Brylcreem and sideburns dead.
    Dead and gone.

Valais

A working river, a working valley,
The gray-green Rhône
Lined with workings, heaps of dust, gravel, cement
And logjams waiting for transport,
Like the island exporting itself to its neighbors one
    barge at a time.

The river, the road, and the railway,
A plait, a tangle, a place of through.
The river not navigable, the boggy valley floor not
    walkable,
The locals came down from the mountains a little way
To site castles on moraine and regulate trade.

Hannibal marched his elephants through here,
    dynamited rocks with vinegar.
Poplars were planted *en passant* by Napoleon's
    Grande Armée
Two hundred some years ago.
Goethe came to visit.
The shade endures.

Rilke was reminded of Spain.
He lived among apricots at Muzot,
Just the other side of the language barrier,
And fixed to be buried with a view of France.
No one knows who I am, were his dying words.

Smells of hay and dung, the murmurs of subtle
    conversation.
Next door are tax-efficient sheep.
The underground chicken palace like CERN
Or a discreet gun emplacement.
The lights come on when we appear, and go off after
    we're gone.

Larchwood and rye bread, chocolate and slate,
Dried beef and stone
All one striated substance,
The staff of life breaking explosively, crumblingly,
If it breaks at all

A stash of daunting verticals,
A washing machine delivered by helicopter
Winched down into the Renaissance casbah.
Time was, a man had to carry his donkey across his
    shoulders up a cliff,
Now everything is tunnel fodder.

Electricity and water come piped through the
    mountains,
The vineyards get a sousing under great rainbow arcs,
Who wouldn't want to die in a thirteenth-century tower
With light sensors and cold running water
Off the hills and a chill in the sunny air of the
    contemporary archaic.

November

for Jamie Buchan

Eine Krähe hackt der anderen [nicht] die Augen aus.
GERMAN PROVERB(S)

Crows on oaks and cranes and cooling towers,
the sky cracking up, and crows investigating
the cream of whatever crust cracks yellow, milling
early birds, Styrofoam beaker of coffee,
refill, refill, and a spot of red-eye gravy.

(leaving Bonn)

Gottfried Benn, c. 1916

I'd rather speak it than write it, rather mutter it than
    speak it
(disobliging spiffy mutter that no one would understand)

how a man—the thing stiffened; the rogue state
familiarly engorged, bristling, crystalline; Myrmidon
    formation,

Schlieffen plan; Prussia the North Korea of the age,
four wars in fifty years, colonies in the Pacific every-
    where not nailed down in 1880—

and our man, himself to himself, the run of eleven
    rooms,
potters, if he cares to (not even *Uniformpflicht*),
    in pajamas and cardigan

neither coward nor conchie, not stricken with disorder,
    disaffection, good fortune,
or even medicine (medicine his sicknote), just
    immeasurable distance,

distance and *froideur*, an antipathy to concerted action
    and human history
beyond the dreams of Keaton or Trakl or Archimedes
    or Schwejk,

smokes and thinks and writes (*béguinage*, he calls it)
in his personal monastery behind the lines in plucky
    little Belgium.

Ostsee

—The water deepens to iodine from brown.

What is there to wait for? The gulls to get bored
of their bouncy slick offshore. The sun to break through
   the qwerty clouds.
The entire coast to make more hagstones, amber,
   jellyfish.
The sand martins to file themselves away in their
   cliffside tenements.
Or the cropped blonde to come back along the beach
with her mystery rucksack and impenetrable wrap-
   arounds,
her superbly articulated deltoids under the black wife-
   beater

—to iodine from brown.

Auden

but you would see faces that were worth a second look
GOTTFRIED BENN

It was another world, the world of turned collars and
    polished shoes,
Hairbrushes once a week laid facedown in what I
    thought was a specific
But was only a weak solution of shampoo in lukewarm
    water,
Jerseys were roughed up with a kind of knuckleduster
    of Sellotape,
Suitcases wore characterful labels and tags on their
    heavy, leather-effect cardboard

Who can imagine such a world not of cares, but of care,
Once we set ourselves to become unpressed, casualized,
    short-run, drip-dry,
Encased in thinking synthetics or flash suits, the human
    fiddler crab and his device
Emerging together from nail bars and tanning studios
    and whitening salons
Like so many gigolos, soccer managers, politicians,
    or molls,

Wearing our fewer, simpler, less restrictive garments
    more shabbily or dressily,
Having our manicures, our teeth whitened, our hair and
    beards repurposed
Every other day, owning either fewer things or they
    were let go to seed,

So intent on our personal grooming, we neglected
   *im*personal grooming,
The care extended beyond ourselves, the aura of
   solicitude surrounding our appurtenances,

The world of facecloths and napkin rings and coal
   scuttles
And coir hall carpets and brass stair rods and milk jugs
   and powdered mustard
And shoe trees and tie racks and plumped down
   pillows and cufflinks and weskits and hats
And hardbound children's books for our hardbound
   children
And malt vinegar and baking soda to take off the worst
   of the dirt,

How careless, cheap, and profligate we have become,
We have stopped shaving against the grain and in cold
   water,
We didn't eat or drink in the street in those days, flawed
   and freckled
An apple was taken for what it was, an undistinguished
   thing and a privilege,
Not chemistry at the top of its game, ester baby,
   breathing perfume and yet found fault with.

In Western Mass.

What do I remember of those strange episodic parts
   of my life.
What they nowadays call outliers. Someone put them
   in brackets.

(Who put them in brackets? I wanted them to go on.)

A dwindling fall, pumpkins, marriage, winter.
The Pioneer Valley. The roaring American convection
   heating.

The fluff off our flannel sheets getting everywhere.
You wrote something about the number of windows.

Was it a lot? You seemed to think it was a lot.

Once, an owl huddled there, pecked at by small birds.
It was daytime and just beginning to snow. Such a
   picture of misery.

Me in my blue shirt, and James's tie. A frog
hopped over my boot. It seemed like luck. Then the
   threshold.

I don't remember kitchen, entertainment center,
   bathroom—
just those cream flannel sheets rubbed and blown
   to lint.

The hereditary medievalist downstairs proclaiming:
    I have seniority in the car park.
The clever, clueless voice in workshop, hazarding:
    is it the voice of coffee.

The black tremulous Jules Feiffer chenille dress you
    married in. Ah, me.

End of the Pier Show

It was—what?—
the triumph of hope
over experience.
But what triumph
(and what hope)?

The continued display
of a kind of unreasonable
fortitude, the man—
Beowulf—stooping
to pick his severed head

off the sawdust, and doing it
again and again.
And she, the woman,
sold, to her mind,
on love

as a kind of motor syrup—
a green linctus—
that was slowly replacing
her blood.
Perhaps lycanthropy.

A pessimistic sublime.
They had made
their bed and they
were jolly well
going to lie in it.

The woman's persistent
complaint that
it wasn't a life,
the man shrugging,
going away, battening down,

daring her to do worse,
if not her worst.
Siege conditions.
And she bringing out
in him strange abysms

of new behavior.
Everything went
so peculiarly,
spectacularly skewed.
They were fascinated

by what they seemed
to have contained.
Unspoolings of truths.
Such dire sayings
of hers. Such vehemence

out of his mouth.
Just as well really
his doggish gloom
met her prickliness
halfway.

Attritional chafe,
chafe, bridle
and chafe, and, periodically,
a grin and tears.
Her good will

expressed itself
in a strange persistence
of affection that he
not unreasonably supposed
would last forever.

(It wasn't to do with him,
was it?)
When it stopped,
he didn't believe it.
He didn't know what to do.

He went hunting around
for the trip switch
that had made this darkness,
this withdrawal.
(Alas, he was never much

of an electrician.)
What happened
to their lovely
puppet theater,
their grand knockabout?

Poem

When all's said and done, there's still
the joyful turning toward you
that feels like the oldest, warmest, and quite
   possibly
best thing in me that I must stifle,
almost as if you were dead,
or I.

Lisburn Road

Ah, if one could at least live like that, not at odds with things
GEORGE SEFERIS

A few yards of vinyl records, well-thumbed,
Under the cistern that sometimes overflows over the
    front door in London,
The drips giving visitors Legionnaire's disease. Books in
    four countries,
The same books. No turntable. None of this is a boast.

Boots, sweaters, jeans, from pre-designer days.
Papers, birth certificate, dead passports, their corners
    docked,
My degree, my decree.
Unopened letters from my mother.

Three sets of taxes, old boarding passes,
Coins, bundled stationery envelopes that are stuck
    down or won't stick.
The whatever world of passwords, streaming, and
    clouds—
Oh, streams and clouds by.

A trunk holding a suitcase holding a holdall,
The travel equivalent of the turducken,
Moth-eaten to buggery.
Children's clothes, Oshkosh, never worn.

Two paintings by a man called Smith, American in
    Paris, or Brit in New York,
One by "Puck" Dachinger, a black canted nude in a
    pink camisole,
With a stove in the corner, scratched with the back of
    the brush:
Ravings from internment on the Isle of Man.

Blood on one of the doors, peach on one of the walls
    (don't ask).
Two plastic bottles of yellowing *samogon* mezcal
From Mexico, sealed with extra twists of plastic.
Imagine traveling with liquids.

Afghan rugs. A reamer, a garlic press.
A funny cup. The *Porky Prime Cut* greetings etched in
    the lead-off grooves,
When not only did you listen to records,
You held them up to the light and read them.

Motet

It's naphtha now you're gone
a sudden apprehension of squalor
the unflowering cardamom plant
gummy with syrup and flies
sour footsmell in the rumpled quilt
a wilted squadron of paper airplanes
ready to take me after you.

Ebenböckstrasse

for my mother

A plaster—piece of sticking plaster—on the wall
Where the doorknob of the cold-water bathroom door
    might hit.
Has hit. A bruise in the other kind of plaster, a dent.
Mend and make do. Guest bathroom, if you will.

It never gets any better; just an embarrassing display
    of solicitude.
A naked concern with wear, like Mylar or antimacassar.
The basin still too small for one hand to wash the other.
A crust of soap. No one's died, at least not recently.

One playpen in the living room, penal, receiving.
Obsolescent photographs of grandchildren.
Small sticky fingerprints. An actual cobweb in my
    cobwebby hair.
Knickknacks no one understands trembling for their
    lives.

Lake Isle

Get me a place on Danube Street, I want to live
on Danube Street, or if not there, then Ann would do
    almost as well,
between the padlocked private gardens (no dogs
    no ball games)
and the barranca, the sanction and the delimited
    amenity.

Mindless wood pigeons bleat like unanswered
    telephones.
Nothing so douce as sandstone in a granite town,
a town monstered by gulls and sunspots and unkempt
    dogs,
softened in any case from when I lived here fifty years
    ago,

when, taking my life in my hands,
I walked to school to save a few shillings bus fare,
beside a Styrofoam stream past drinks cans and jobbies
    and the occasional
murdered foreign student, but not too many.

Where the walls are scarred with YMD (for Young
    Mental Drylaw),
and the streets on Fridays are blustery with witty
    drunks,
and beautiful grant-maintained schoolgirls
tuck into beastly food with savage appetites.

I want to have wooden shutters and specimen plants,
Georgian casements (the only artifact I'd countenance
    from two millennia),
and ten fine days a year, fossicking at home in a
    cardigan
while my fellow professionals are all at work.

I want to take my place as a nationally—make that
    notionally—
known professor, among investment advisers and plastic
    surgeons,
where there are always builders making improvements
    or repairs,
and the cobbles play merry hell with the bottles on the
    milk floats.

Seagulls, Italian Style

[where engineering meets design] their creams and tans
a conscious color statement, a finer, flashier glide,
a bigger entrance and a bigger entrancement,
volplaning wardrobes always newly back from the
    cleaners,

neither "scroungers of the empyrean" nor "nibblers of
    edible stars"
their minds on higher things (or lower things),
cashmere sleeves dangle-draped over their shoulders,
annulments in their man bags, foulard, eyewear, metal
    bangles.

Venice Beach

Annihilating all that's made
To a green thought in a green shade
ANDREW MARVELL

Things had better work here, because here, beneath
that immense bleached sky, is where we run out of
continent.

JOAN DIDION

These are all thoughts—of course. At the edge of the
    ocean with nowhere to go,
the nearest land three thousand miles away and under
    different management,

the diving sun another thirty thousand times that, there
    is no reality,
only these parlous notions, messages, statements, stylings
    on the edge of extinction.

Little petillas. A kind of spontaneous zoo of human
    recency and arrival
and promontory variorum. Imprudent combover
    thoughts,

rigid and proud eye-catching false thoughts, little jiggling
    thoughts,
intricate braided beard thoughts the product of much
    misplaced patience,

product placement thoughts (which are rather elementary,
and are almost a contradiction in terms), unlike myriad
    highly evolved

dog thoughts (no mutts here), pushing a baby in a three-
    wheeled stroller
while running very hard in no shirt and sixpack
    thoughts,

this a development on the now-obsolete egg and paddle
(what it does to the infant to be impelled at such a rate
    into the future

while facing backwards like an Aeroflot passenger is not
    recorded—
not that forward is necessarily better), high-concept
    silky-swishing Afghan hound thoughts,

intrusive bum thoughts, hapless and homeless pan-
    handler thoughts
(a Smarte Carte loaded with undesirables never far to seek),

low-slung belly-dragging beagle thoughts little better
than the serpent in the Bible, holding hands Adam and
    Eve thoughts,

foot-shuffling Zimmer frame thoughts, "revolution in
    mobility" wheelchair and gravel thoughts,
pushed by most likely an illegal attendant borderline
    thoughts,

candy striped T-shirt and shorts thoughts, cut-off
    thoughts,
paired with sometimes nothing more than a bikini top,
    those three-quarter-length,

thin, and probably amphibious trousers, worn without
    socks, that men go in for,
suggestive of adaptability and resourcefulness thoughts,

standard overloud mobile thoughts, ("our relationship
   is . . ."),
lying immobile on the grass on your back mobile
   thoughts

(these are different), tourist thoughts, an unexpected
   preponderance of Russian thoughts
(though with residential qualifications), borscht belt
   leopard-skin thoughts

dripping with gold and eccentric lamentations, dog and
   baby both thoughts
(these last thought to be ideally balanced), high-
   stepping poodle thoughts

like a four-wheel drive with little intelligence in rough
   country,
furiously texting in the glare with all thumbs to the
   pump thoughts,

being at least half elsewhere, baseball cap thoughts rife
   with determination,
slightly dated straw hat thoughts, reverse baseball cap
   also thoughts.

Midterms

Those no-treads. Scott and Tom and Scott Scott and
    Tom Tom,
wealth creator or small billionaire or lawyer or even,
    even woman,
groomed for the succession from yea high, or there on
    sudden impulse
or empaneled cosmeticists' and focus groups' say-so,
committed to working (or porking) across the aisle,
    "humbled"
(read insufferably puffed up) to "serve" (*recte* rob and
    enfeeble
and generally mal-administer) his/her flyover state (its
    name here _____):
the great, the great, the greatest the world has never
    seen
in—uh—the entire history of the world.

Higher Learning

for Sarah Trudgeon and Aaron Thier

"We monetize the university.
Raid the pension fund, lease out the classrooms,
    put coin slots on the phones and copy machines,
and we throw money at the football team, the
    basketball team, the track team, all the other teams.
Sport deepens the Crocodile brand. Sport kicks
    communities and builds ass. You can shove the rest.

We casualize the support staff. Who's scared of a few
    roaches and spiders.
We empty the bins once a week, then once a month.
    Are we serious about paperless learning or not?
We stop the water fountains. Don't replace bulbs,
    call it green, and save thousands.
To think big, you've got to dare to think small.

We pause the elevators, let the profs find their own way
    downstairs
by the light of their towering intellects—or, more likely,
    their smartphones.
Bunch of limey faggots. Underpaid, undersexed, and
    underwear.
Or, as I believe they like to say over there, 'pants.'

We get some proper K Street chops into our fund-raising
    effort.
Personalized databases. Twitter feeds. Birthday messages.
    Con-dolences and -gratulations.

A little complimentary merchandise goes a long way.
    Preformatted wills.
Candlelight giggle-o dinner dates with Old Croquettes.

We hike the fees and we re-prioritize.
It's what you do in a race to the bottom.
We lay on handmaidens and academic tutors and
    personal chefs for our MVPs—
everything, and the great lunks still pass out at traffic
    lights.

We do a heavy concentration on STEM subjects,
plus microbiology, medicine, law, and one other.
Entrepreneur.
The rest can go wither. What are we here for—
    educating citizens?!

We free up tenure. We deaccession the library.
You don't need books to cut and paste, I always say.

We boost distance learning. Streaming lectures. Log on
    and goof off.
Overspill classes. Computer grading. Multiple choice.
Redefine the contact hour. Redefine the degree.
Virtuality is the new reality.

We put in a Gap and a Walmart, and call them book-
    shops.
We sell Pepsi one university-wide monopoly franchise
    in perpetuity, and Taco Bell another.
and in general we take a leaf out of the contemporary
    airport:
a shopping center with half a runway attached.

We award our sports coaches *ius primae noctis* (for
    wins only),
plus 40,000-square-foot pasteboard-and-marble
    mansions on prime lakeside real estate,
with green lights at the end of their private piers.
Throw in a motorboat and some stables, or else we're
    uncompetitive.

We put up a new building a week—prospective parents
like to see that stuff—and we sell on the naming rights
    to the old ones.
They plow up cemeteries, don't they?
Nothing's forever. Go Crocks."

Less Truth

kneedeep in foaming status quo
HANS MAGNUS ENZENSBERGER

more denials, more prevarication, more #real hashtags
and pop-ups and calculating interesticles, more clickbait,
more straight-faced, bare-faced, faceless, baseless
counter-allegations, more red herrings, crossed fingers,
rehearsed answers, turned tables, impossibilities
before breakfast, more "accepting responsibility," less
    truth.
Lusher menus. Bigger bonuses. Less contrition. More
    shamelessness.
Less truth.

Silly Season, 2015

Money is speech. Firms have feelings. The People's Re-
    public of Facebook
is offended by that woman's pseudonym,
takes a copy of her passport to have her account made
    out to her real identity.

Your bank card is good for drawing cash, but
not for a balance or a statement. The Greeks, mean-
    while,
revert to barter. One wolf cries "terrorist!"

and sheep come from miles around to applaud a (Kurd-
    ish) boy being savaged.
(It's called NATO.) A list of NSA search terms
is so confidential, it can be shown to one person, if that.

Beate Zschäpe, on trial for the past two years for her
    part
in the racial murder of ten people, shares giggles
with her latest defense lawyer (28), cold shoulders

the other three. The accused bench is like a box at the
    opera,
there she is, popping a cachou into the new boy's
    mouth, cynosure, flash of cleavage.
Wagner directs Wagner. Disparities widen; "scissors" is
    the German term of art.

Cities fill up/empty out (your choice) with "buy to
    leave" property.
Countries not busily pursuing their dissolution (UK,
    Belgium) harden themselves.
Walls go up against Serbia, Mexico, Palestine. A large
    body of water is of course (Australia) ideal.

Donald Trump pioneers the quick-drying comb-under.
The Republicans come up this time with (digit sum:
    seven) sixteen dwarves.
Never mind the quality, feel the narrowness.

The weather breaks records every which way; traffic
    reports—
miles of *Stau*—go on forever. Railways lose money hand
    over fist, but continue
their policy of neurotically expressive pricing (no two
    journeys the same).

The Chinese stock exchange gets all kittenish at a cost
    of trillions.
America is good for an atrocity a week ("gun violence"),
    and doesn't get it.
Brazenness or apology: a style choice. Putin is a figure
    from Artaud or Genet;

"Sepp" Blatter wins and postdates his flounce out of
    FIFA; "el Chapo"
burrows out of a high-security Mexican prison on a
    rail-mounted motorbike.
Lame-duck Obama goes to Africa to preach the virtues
    of term limits.

Human rights lawyers disappear like old snow or coral
    reefs or old-growth forests.
Most constitutional arrangements are subject to review,
most trade is with China. Nothing trumps (trumps!)
    immediate gratification.

Governments continue to attempt to refine their
    populations.
The new instrument of domestic policy is the F-16,
used by Syria, and now, three years later, by Turkey as
    well.

Saudi Arabia apes the U.S.; a "loose" alliance "of the
    willing" bombs Yemen every day for months.
Whole families up sticks and emigrate to ISIS, if they
    can find it, or failing that ISIL.
Religions have feelings. Cartoons aren't funny. Speech
    costs.

The Case for Brexit

for Frederick Seidel

I dropped my new shoes in the stream, thinking perhaps
They would get there before me, like two drowned Jews
Trundling along the seabed to Jerusalem. My immigrant
    parents lost patience and thrashed me.
The best thing that ever happened to me was on the boat.
I've no idea what it was. Then Tilbury. Or Harwich.
    Or Southampton.

I got eggshells crushed with lemon juice for the calcium
    and its better absorption.
I got buttered bread with a little bitter chocolate grated
    over it.
I got glabrous soured milk with cinnamon and sugar.
I got kohlrabi and celeriac and other nonexistent
    vegetables,
Like so many chimeras and hippogriffs.

I got *Kinderkaffee* from malted barley, and *Katarzynki*
    from Mr. Continental, but only on Thursdays.
I got vermillion worm medicine, with bitter lemon
That didn't begin to take away the color or the taste.
The four of us round the table. We all had to do it.
    It was like a suicide pact.
It was the winter of '63, the Plath winter. I barked for
    months.

I juggle the numbers, the way I sang my times tables
On the swing. (They are all I have in the world.)
   The sevens, the nines.
They mostly begin with the scalene 19—. I swing them
   around, sling them and swing them.
Lennon and Kennedy and punk and the Wall and the
   moon.
Big numbers, jagged numbers, like someone with very
   heavy weights.

I invented sepia. Sepia came for me. Something
   discolored
Behind me, in my past, like a hobbled Clovis ad.
   Our charlady smelled so terrible,
My father smoked a pipe ("Fair Play") after she was
   gone. My young mother still giggled.
She and my father played badminton on the street at
   night.
You could read the *Times* past eleven. (You could read
   the *Times*.)

School uniforms, playground fights. Goalposts. Polar
   ghosts. British bulldogs.
I should have liked to be called Roger or Arthur. The
   bully Brian Lorry pummeled and pummeled.
All Trutex or Aertex. Caps. Striped ties and the striped
   elastic belt with the snake-mouth hook.
Melrose, RHS, Loretto, George Watson's, Boys' *and*
   Girls'—all mauled us.
I was at bat for days without scoring a run.

Practically everything was a shibboleth. Harwich was a
    trick.
Berwick was a trick. Worcester was a trick. Geoffrey
    was a trick. I didn't know Sundays were no-go.
My home German was compared to a serendipitous
    knowledge of Welsh;
I knew better: it was less. My only friend, McVicar, had
    a Greek mother. Maybe Clytemnestra.
They moved further north, so that he could be with
    Prince Charles.

Coventry

Two of us in the chandeliered room, the only ones
not speaking to anyone. Me and a man twice my age,
which unfortunately puts him at a hundred and twelve.

He might be Ernst Jünger's older brother, a frazzled
   cherub with a war wound.
He has worked out that, if you are to be alone,
then like a suicide bomber in the middle of a cluster
   of people.

Sweeps of radar. A turning circle of sorts. Ultra-
   approachable.
I imagine his hearing aid off. Procuring the
   companionable human jostle.
Shoulders. Feet. Excuse me.

On Forgetting

IQ of 145 and can't remember?
TROUBLING HISTORIC BROADSHEET ADVERTISEMENT

"Empiricism" has been gone far more often than not;
I think I originally learned it in my teens.
Now I sometimes find it by alphabetizing, but most of
    the time it's gone and stays gone.
I don't know if I dislike it because I can't remember it,
    or I can't remember it because I dislike it.
It's as though it's on permanent loan somewhere.
    Someone else's problem.

I don't know what would alarm me—really alarm me.
"Galicia" was gone. Both Galicias. "Boarding pass"
    recently disappeared for a while.
I keep a firm hold on "ocarina" and "Hoffmeister,"
eschewing "Hoffman" and "Hofmeister," that tacky
    1980s lager when German became respectable.
I do *Corona, Corona* and "Corinna, Corinna" and la
    Coruña. That's the *el camino* one.

I walked thirty blocks the wrong way down Derision.
The ordered numbers seemed to make no sense.
I was unclear about Hamilton and Harrison. Weren't
    they presidents?
If not, why not? Confound it, I didn't know which way
    was up or west.
I hoped the Post Office might be a Travelodge, where I
    finally posted my letter.

"Abstemious" was gone for years, now I keep hold of it
by tethering it to "facetious." What if "facetious" goes?
    Imagine not knowing "facetious."
It would help to have a crocodile, a street of crocodiles.
"I was here yesterday, and I lost a brown glove,"
says a loud voice in a bar, not mine. Or not yet.
    Actually, it was a blue glove.

I get my Magyars mixed up. Was it Zsuzsa Rakovsky
    or Agnes Nemes Nagy? A or Z?
"Deborah" has displaced "Dorothea," or was it vice
    versa. Now where are they?
I disappear into my room to look for a book,
and emerge hours later with the wrong one, or with
    none at all.
Tell me, is it "singular universality" or "simple
    unavailability"?

Tiger-striped spectacles and a lazy eye.
"How about I come over and make you forget all about
    him."
That's not me either, that's for something called Grub-
    hub,
over a 10,000 calorie picture of à la mode or Miracle
    Whip. There's comfort.
Probably, come to think about it, the "him" would be
    Grubby Hubby.

My spelling isn't what it was. I talk when I have the
    words.
They are not always there when I talk.
I'm not sure if that makes me long-winded or delphic.
    Perhaps both.
I remember, I wrote "apotropaically" once,
I wrote "anamorphosis," I wrote "aporia."

It's 12/12/12. *Rien ne va plus.* 'Bout them Mayans.
The Pope has tweeted assurance, or his astronomers
    have. Sweet comfort.
Sweet tweet comfort. It's not la Coruña at all, it's
    Compostela. Ah, Stella.
Stella or Vanessa, make a decision. The pilgrims with
    their scallop shells of quiet,
their *Jakobsmuscheln*, on their hats. Strange place for
    a shell, no.

(Chicago)

Cooking for One

I put five small potatoes in a saucepan,
hold it under the cold tap
till they're covered with water,
add a squirt of washing-up liquid.
—There's a man who likes his life.

Idyll

The windows will reflect harder, blacker, than before,
and fresh cracks will appear in the yellow brick.

There is no milkman or paper boy, but presumably
the lurid pizza flyers and brassy offers of loans

will continue to drop through the letter box.
The utilities will be turned off one by one,

as the standing orders keel over or lose their address,
though there was never that much cooking or bathing or

phoning went on here anyway—the fridge will stop its
    buzz,
the boiler its spontaneous combusting—till there is
    nothing

but a mustiness of gas. The dust will coil and thicken
ultimately to hawsers around pipes and wires;

ever more elaborate spiders' webs will sheet off the
    corners;
rust stains and mildew and rot will spread chromatically

below the holes in the roof, radiate from the radiators;
eventually mosses and small grasses and even admirable

wildflowers, hell, an elder or buddleia, push their heads
through the chinks between the boards; a useless volume
    of books—

who could ever read that many—will keep the moths
    entertained,
generations of industrious wood lice and silverfish

will leave their corpses on the clarty work surfaces,
and a pigeon or two will hook its feet over the
    tarnished sink

and brood vacantly over its queenly pink toes.